SCHIRMER'S LIBRARY
OF MUSICAL CLASSICS

Vol. 101

ROBERT SCHUMANN

Op. 15

Scenes from Childhood

For the Piano

Edited by

HAROLD BAUER

T0055394

G. SCHIRMER, Inc.

DISTRIBUTED BY

HAL•LEONARD®
CORPORATION

7777 W. BLUEMOUND RD. P.O. BOX 13819 MILWAUKEE, WI 53213

PREFACE

TO

SCENES FROM CHILDHOOD, Op. 15

The origin of "Kinderszenen" . (Scenes from Childhood) lies apparently in a chance remark of Clara's that Robert sometimes seemed to her like a child. He was willing to accept this appraisal of his personality and wrote her shortly afterwards that he had composed about thirty little pieces from which thirteen were to be selected and called "Kinderszenen" .

"You will like them", he added, "but you must forget that you are a virtuoso. They make a great impression—especially on myself!—when I play them." He was indignant when the composition, on its publication, was belittled by the well-known Berlin music critic, Heinrich Rellstab, who suggested that a musical imitation of the actions of a child could hardly be taken seriously. "I have never heard of anything so stupid", wrote Robert. "It is precisely the other way round. I do not deny, of course, that I was thinking of children when I composed the pieces— Ottilie Voigt's big blue eyes go so well with them, for instance—but the titles were given afterwards and these titles are, in fact, nothing but directions for the performance of the music."

As indicated in the editor's preface to "Album for the Young", Op. 68, the "Scenes from Childhood" were to be considered "Reminiscences" whereas the pieces in the "Album" should be regarded as "Anticipations".

What became of the rest of the group of pieces referred to in Robert's letter to Clara? They were laid aside, in the present writer's opinion, to be published many years later in the two collections entitled respectively "Bunte Blätter", Op. 99, and "Albumblätter", Op. 124.

The "Kinderszenen" bear no dedication, although it seems certain that the work was first intended to be inscribed to Schumann's close friend, Anton Zuccalmaggio

                                                              H. B.

Scenes from Childhood
Kinderszenen
13 Piano Pieces

Edited by
Harold Bauer

Robert Schumann, Op. 15

1. About Strange Lands and People
Von fremden Ländern und Menschen

40939 r×

2. Curious Story
Kuriose Geschichte

Allegro giojoso ♩ = 132

3. Blindman's buff

Hasche-Mann

Allegro scherzando ♩ = 116

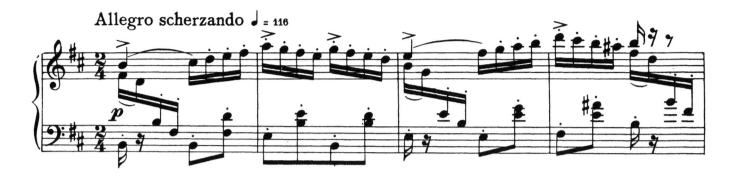

4. Pleading Child

Bittendes Kind

5. Perfectly Contented
Glückes genug

40939

6. Important Event

Wichtige Begebenheit

Allegro marziale ♩ = 120

7. Reverie
Träumerei

*Original

8. At the Fireside

Am Kamin

Allegretto grazioso ♩ = 104

40939

9. The Knight of the Rocking-horse

Ritter vom Steckenpferd

10. Almost too Serious
Fast zu ernst

Moderato, poco rubato ♪ = 100

11. Frightening
Fürchtenmachen

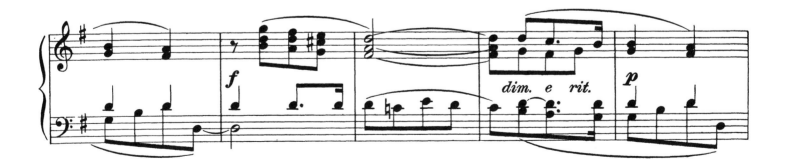

40939

Più mosso ♩ = 132

Meno mosso ♩ = 108   Tempo primo

Più mosso

Tempo primo

12. Child Falling Asleep
Kind im Einschlummern

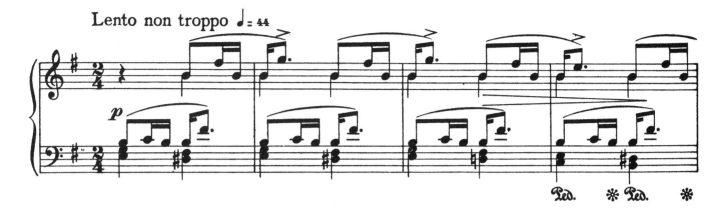

40939

13. The Poet speaks
Der Dichter spricht

Adagio espressivo ♩ = 88

Tempo primo

* Original:

The absence of a qualifying A in the bass, not only here but in the similar cadence eight measures from the end, is totally incomprehensible to the present editor. However, this open space has apparently been left without comment in all other editions.

This, according to Carl Deis, is the interpretation of the composer's peculiar notation.